LA TRAVIATA

ACT I.	ATTO I.

SCENE I—A salon in the house of Violetta; in the back scene is a door, which opens into another salon; there are also side doors; on the left is a fireplace, over which is a mirror. In the centre of the apartment is a dining-table, elegantly laid.

(Violetta, seated on a couch is conversing with the Doctor and some friends, whilst others are receiving the guests who arrive, among whom are the Baron, and Flora on the arm of the Marquis.)

Chorus 1—Past already's the hour of appointment—
    You are tardy.

Chorus 2—We played deep at Flora's,
    And while playing the hours flew away.

Violetta—Flora, and kind friends, the night is before us.
    Other pleasures we here will display.
        (Goes to meet them.)
    'Mid the wine-cups the hours pass more gaily.

Flora
Marquis } Can you there find enjoyment?

Violetta—I strive to;
    Yes, to pleasure I yield, and endeavor
    With such remedies illness to stay.

All—Yes! enjoyment will lengthen our days.

SCENE II—The same. Gaston and Alfred enter. Servants are busy about the table.

Gaston—In Alfred Germent, fairest lady,
    Another behold, who esteems you
    There are few friends like him; he a treasure.

Violetta—Thanks, dear Viscount, for so great a pleasure.
    (She gives her hand to Alfred, who kisses it.)

Marquis—Dear Alfred!

Alfred—Kind Marquis!
        (They shake hands.)

Gaston—I told you
        (to Alfred).
    That combined here are friendship and pleasure.
    (During this dialogue the servants have placed the viands upon the table.)

Violetta—All is ready?
        (A servant bows assent.)
    My dear friends, be seated;
    'Tis at the banquet that each heart unfolds.

Chorus—Thou has wisely the maxim repeated,
    Cure for trouble the wine-cup still holds.
    (They seat themselves, Violetta between Alfred and Gaston, and opposite to them Flora, the Marquis, and the Baron; the rest take their seats promiscuously; there is a momentary silence, during which the dishes are passed round, and Violetta and Gaston converse in an undertone.)

SCENA I—Salotto in casa di Violetta; nel fondo è la porta che mette ad altra sala; ve ne sono altre due laterali: a sinistra un caminetto con sopra uno specchio. Nel mezzo è una tavola riccamente imbandita.

(Violetta seduta sur un divano sta discorrendo col Dottore, e con alcuni amici, mentre altri vanno ad incontrare quelli che sopraggiungono, tra' quali sono il Barone e Flora al braccio del Marchese.)

Coro 1.—Dell' invito trascora è gia l' ora—
    Voi tardaste.

Coro 2—Giocammo da Flora,
    E giocando quell' ore volar.

Violetta—Flora, amici, la notte che resta
    D'altre gioie qui fate brilla—
        (andando ore incontre,
    Fra le tazze è più viva la festa.

Flora
Marchese } E goder voi potrete?

Violetta—Lo voglio;
    Alla danza m'affido, ed io soglio
    Con tal farmaco i mali sopir.

Tutti—Sì, la vita s'addoppia al gioir.

SCENA II—Detti, il Visconte Gastone di Letorieres, Alfredo Germont; servi affaccendati intorno all mensa.

Gastone—In Alfredo Germont, o signora,
    Ecco un altro che molto vi onora;
    Pochi amici a lui simili sono.

Violetta—Mio Visconte, mercè di tal dono.
    (dà la mano ad Alfredo, che gliela bacia.)

Marchese—Caro Alfredo!

Alfredo—Marchese!
        (si stringono la mano.)

Gastone—T'ho detto
        (ad Alfredo.)
    L'amistà qui s' intreccia al diletto.
    (I servi frattanto avranno imbandite le vivande.)

Violetta—Pronto è il tutto?
        (un servo accenna che sì.)
    Miei cari, sedete
    E al convito che s' apre ogni cor.

Tutti—Ben diceste—le cure segrete
    Fuga sempre l'amico licor.
    (Siedono in modo che Violetta resti tra Alfredo e Gastone; di fronte vi sarà Flora, il Marchese ed il Barone; gli altri siedono a piacere. Vi ha un momento di silenzio; frattanto passano i piatti, e Violetta e Gastone parlano sotto voce tra loro.)

3

Gaston—Thou'art the sole thought of Alfred.
(to VIOLETTA).

Violetta—Art jesting?

Gaston—Thou wert ill, an each day in distress
He came to ask thy condition.

Violetta—Be silent;
No, I am naught to him.

Gaston—I deceive not.
(to ALFRED).

Violetta—Is it true then? Can it be? Ah, I know not.
(sighing).

Alfred—Yes, it is true.
(to ALFRED).

Violetta—Grateful thanks, then, I give you.
(to the BARON).
You, dear Baron, were not so enamored.

Baron—But 'tis only a year I have known you.

Violetta—And Alfred a few minutes only.
(softly to the BARON).

Flora—'Twould be better if you had not spoken.
(softly to FLORA).

Baron—For this youth I've no liking.

Flora—But why?
As for me, now, he pleases me well.
(to ALFRED).

Gaston—Thou art silent hast nothing to offer?

Marquis—Madame alone has the power to arouse him.
(fills the glass of ALFRED).

Violetta—I will fill, then, like Hebe!

Alfred—And like her.
I proclaim thee immortal.

All—We pledge thee!
(to the BARON).

Gaston—Can you not, in this moment of pleasure,
Give a toast, or a gay tuneful measure?
(the BARON declines).
(to ALFRED).
Then wilt thou—

All—Yes, yes, a drinking song.

Alfred—I've no inspiration.

Gaston—Art thou not then a singer?
(to VIOLETTA).

Alfred—Will it please you?

Violetta—Yes.
(rising).

Alfred—Yes, Then I yield.

Marquis—Pay attention!

All—Yes, attention we'll pay!

Gastone—Sempre Alfredo a voi pensa.

Violetta—Scherzate?

Gastone—Egra foste, e ogni dì con affanno
Qui volò, di voi chiese.

Violetta—Cessate.
Nulla son io per lui.

Gastone—Non v' inganno.
(ad ALFREDO.)

Violetta—Vero è dunque?—Onde ciò? Nol comprendo.
(sospirande.)

Alfredo—Sì, egli è ver.

Violetta—Le mie grazie vi rendo.
(al BARONE.)
Voi, barone, non feste altrettanto.

Barone—Vi conosco da un anno soltanto.

Violetta—Ed ei solo da qualche minuto.
(piano al BARONE).

Flora—Meglio fora, se aveste taciuto.
(piano a FLORA.)

Barone—M'è increscioso qquel giovin.

Flora—Perchè?
A me invece simpatico egli è.
(ad ALFREDO.)

Gastone—E tu dunque non apri più bocca?
(a VIOLETTA)

Marchese—E a madama che scuoterlo tocca
(mesc ad ALFREDO).

Violetta—Saro l'Ebe che versa.

Alfredo—E ch' io bramo
Immortal come quella.
(con galanteria.)

Tutti—Beviamo.

Gastone—O Barone, nè un verso, nè un viva
Troverete in quest' ora giuliva?
(BARONE accenna di nò.)
(ad ALFREDO.)
Dunque a te.

Tutti—Sì, sì, un brindisi.

Alfredo—L'estro non m'arride.

Gastone—E non se' tu maestro?
(a VIOLETTA)

Alfredo—Vi fia grato?

Violetta—Sì.
(si alza.)

Alfredo—Sì?—L'ho in cor.

Marchese—Dunque attenti.

Tutti—Sì, attenti al cantor.

LIBIAMO NE' LIETI—*A BUMPER WE'LL DRAIN* (Alfred)

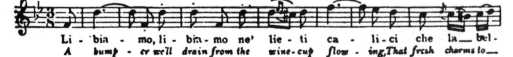

Li - bia - mo, li - bia - mo ne' lie - ti ca - li - ci che la___ bel -
A bump - er we'll drain from the wine-cup flow - ing,That fresh charms to___

4

LA TRAVIATA

lez - za in - fio - ra, e la _____ fug - ge - vol, fug - gé - vol o -
beau - ty is lend - ing, O'er fleet - ing mo - ments, so quick - ly end.

- ra sin - ne - bri - i a vo - lut - - tà. Li - biam ne' dol - ci _____
ing, Gay pleas - ure a - lone should ___ reign. We'll drink the thrill - ing _____

fre - mi - ti che su - sci - ta l'a - mo - re, poi - chè quel l'oc - chio al
ec - sta - sies, That love ex - cites with *.. in us, When her bright eye doth ___

co - re on - ni - po - ten - te _____ và _____ Li - bia - mo, a - mo - re à -
win us, And ev - 'ry heart re - tain _____ A bump - er to love, mid the

mor fra i ca - - li - ci più cal - di ___ ba - ci - a vrà.
wine - cups flow - ing, Fresh warmth will our ___ pleas - ures re - gain.

Ah! to love, 'mid wine-cups flowing
New delight our joys will gain.

Violetta—Surrounded by you, I shall learn to
    lighten
The footsteps of time with gladness;
All of this world is but folly and madness
That is not pleasure gay.
Enjoy the hour, for rapid
The joys of life are flying—
Like summer flow'rets dying—
Improve them while we may!
Enjoy! the present with fervor invites us,
Its flattering call obey.

All—Enjoy then the wine-cup with songs of
    pleasure
That make night so cheerful and smiling,
In this charming paradise, beguiling,
That scarely we heed the day.

        (to ALFRED).
Violetta—The sum of life is pleasure.

        (to VIOLETTA).
Alfred—While still unloved, unloving?

        (to ALFRED).
Violetta—Experience ne'er has taught me.

        (to VIOLETTA).
Alfred—And thus my fate must be.

        (music is heard in another room).
All—What's this?

Violetta—Will you not join the gay group of
    dancers?

All—Oh! a happy thought! We'll gladly join
    them.

Libiamo; amor fra i calici
Più caldi baci avrà.

Violetta—Tra voi, saprò dividere (s' alza.)
Il tempo mio giocondo;
Tutto è follia nel monde
Ciò che non è piacer.
Godiam; fugace e rapido
È il gaudio dell' amore:
È un fior che nasce e muore
Nè più si può goder.
Godiam—c'invita un fervido
Accento lusinghier.

Tutti—Godiam—la tazza e il cantico
Le notti abbella e il riso;
In questo paradiso,
Ne scuopra il nuovo dì.

        ad ALFREDO.)
Violetta—La vita è nel tripudio.

        (a VIOLETTA.)
Alfredo—Quando non s'ami ancora.

        ad ALFREDO.)
Violetta—Nol dite a chi l'ignora.

        (a VIOLETTA.)
Alfredo—E il mio destin così.

        (S' ode musica dall altra sala.)
Tutti—Che è cio.

Violetta—Non gradireste ora le danse?

Tutti—Oh, il gentile pensier!—Tutti accet-
    iamo.

5

Violetta—Then let us enter!

(Approaching the door, VIOLETTA, seized with a sudden faintness, cries out:)
Alas!

All—What ails thee?

Violetta—Nothing, nothing.

All—Why do you pause then?

Violetta—Let's go now.

(Takes a few steps, but is obliged to re-seat herself.)
Oh, Heaven!

All—Again still!

Alfred—Ah! you suffer—

All—Oh, Heaven! what means this?

Violetta—A sudden tremor seized me. Now—
there, pray enter.
(Pointing to the other room.)
I will enjoin you ere long.

All—As you desire, then.
(All pass into the other room, except ALFRED.)

SCENE III—VIOLETTA, ALFRED, afterward GASTON.

(rises and regards herself in a mirror).

Violetta—A me! how pale!
(Turning, she perceives ALFRED).
You here?

Alfred—Are you relieved from recent distress?

Violetta—I'm better!

Alfred—Ah, these gay revels soon will destroy
thee.
Great care is needful—on this depends your
being.

Violetta—Canst thou then aid me?

Alfred—Oh! wert thou mine now, with vigilance
untiring
I'd guard thee with tenderest care.

Violetta—What say'st thou?
Some one, perchance, then cares for me?
(confusedly).

Alfred—No one in all the world doth love you.

Violetta—No one?

Alfred—I, only, love you.

Violetta—Ah! truly!
(laughing).
Your great devotion I had quite forgotten.

Alfred—Dost mock me? Have you a heart then?

Violetta—A heart? Yes—haply—but why do you
thus question

Alfred—Ah, if you had one you wold not thus
trifle with me.

Violetta—Are you then truthful?

Alfred—You, I deceive not.

Violetta—'Tis long, that you have thus loved me?

Alfred—Ah, yes a year now.

Violetta—Usciamo dunque?

(S' avviano alla porta di mezzo ma VIOLETTA
e colta da subito pallore.)
Ohimè!

Tutti—Che avete?

Violetta—Nulla, nulla.

Tutti—Che mai v'arresta?

Violetta—Usciamo.
(Fà qualche passo, ma è obbligata a nuova-
mente ferman e sedere.)
Oh Dio!

Tutti—Ancora!

Alfredo—Voi soffrite.

Tutti—Oh ciel!—Ch'è questo?

Violetta—E un tremito che provo—or là
passate,
(indicando l' altra stanza.)
Tra poco anch' io sarò.

Tutti—Come bramate.
Tutti passano all' altra sala, meno ALFREDO, che
resta indietro.)

SCENA III—VIOLETTA, ALFREDO, e GASTONE, a
tempo.

Violetta—Oh, qual pallor!
(si guarda nello specchio).
Voi qui!
(volgendosi s' accorge d' ALFREDO.)

Alfredo—Cessata è l'ansia, che vi turbò?

Violetta—Sto meglio.

Alfredo—Ah, in cotal guisa v'ucciderete!
Aver v'è d'uopo cura dell' esser
vostro.

Violetta—E lo potrei?

Alfredo—Se mia foste, custode io veglierei
Pe' vostri soavi dì.

Violetta—Che dite?
Ha forse alcuno cura di me?

Alfredo—Perchè nessuno al mondo v'ama.

Violetta—Nessun?

Alfredo—Tranne sol io.

Violetta—Gli è vero!
(ridende.)
Sì grande amor dimenticato avea.

Alfredo—Ridete!—e in voi v' ha un core?

Violetta—Un cor? Sì, forse—e a che lo
richiedete?

Alfredo—Oh, se ciò fosse, non potreste
allora celiar.

Violetta—Dite davvero?

Alfredo—Io non v'inganno.

Violetta—Di molto è che mi amate?

Alfredo—Ah sì, da un anno.

LA TRAVIATA

UN DI FELICE—*ONE DAY. A RAPTURE* (Alfred)

Un di fe-li-ce e-te-re-a mi ba-le na-ste in-nan -
One day a rap-ture e-the-re-al Flash'd on my heart its bright -

te, e da quel di— tre-man-te vis-si d'ig-no-to a-mor.
ness, And, since that day— of light-ness, Life's on-ly aim has been love.

Di quell' a-mor, quell' a-mor— ch'e pal-pi-to dell' u-ni-
Ah, yes, of lore, of the lore— that pal-pi-tates Thro' all the

ver-so, dell' u-ni-ver-so in-te-ro,— mi-ste-ri-o-so, mi-ste-ri-o-so al-
world, thru' cre-a-tion wide, ex-tend-ed; Oh, pow'r mys-te-rious, pow'r yet un-com-pre-

te-ro, cro-ce, cro-ce e de-li-zia, cro-ce e de-li-zia, de-li-zia al cor.
hend-ed; Tor-ment, tor-ment and rap-ture, tor-ment and rap-ture, each do I prove.

Violetta—If this be true, ah! fly from me. Friendship alone I offer, I neither know nor suffer A feeling of such devotion. I am sincere and frank with thee; Look for one warmer, kinder; 'Twill not be hard to find her, Then think no more of me.	*Violetta*—Ah, se ciò è ver, fuggitemi— Pura amistade io v'offro; Amar non sò, nè soffro Di così eroico ardor. Io sono franca, ingenua; Altra cercar devoto— Non arduo troverete Dimentecarmi allor.

Alfred—Oh love, sublime, yet mysterious,
Power ne'er yet comprehended,
Torments and raptures of love!
    (appearing at the door).
	Alfredo—Oh amore misterioso,
	Misterioso altero,
	Croce e delizia al cor
	    (presentandosi sulla porta di mezzo).

Gaston—How now? What here employs you?	*Gastone*—Ebben?—che diavol fate?
Violetta—Trifles and folly.	*Violetta*—Si folleggiava.

Gaston—Ah, that is well. Remain then.
    (goes back).
    (to ALFRED).
	Gastone—Ah, ah!—stà ben—restate.
	    (rientra.)

Violetta—Of love speak we no more. It is
    agreed on?
	Violetta—Amor, dunque, non più—vi garba
	    il patto?

Alfred—I will obey you—farewell.
    (about to depart).
	Alfredo—Io v'obbedisco—Partò.
	    (par andarsene.)

Violetta—Is such your pleasure?
    (takes a flower from her bosom).
    Then take with thee this flow'ret.
	Violetta—A tal giungeste?
	    (si toglie un fiore dal seno.)
	    Prendete questo fiore.

Alfred—And why?	*Alfredo*—Perche?

Violetta—Soon to return it.
    (returning)
	Violetta—Per riportarlo.
	    (tornando.)

Alfred—How soon?	*Alfredo*—Quando?
Violetta—When its gay bloom is faded.	*Violetta*—Quando sarà appassito.

LA TRAVIATA

Alfred—Oh, joy! To-morrow!

Violetta—'Tis well—to-morrow!

Alfred—I am a las so happy!
    (seizes the flower with transport).

Violetta—You still declare you love me?

Alfred—How much I love thee!
    (going).

Violetta—You go then.

Alfred—Yes, love!
    (returns and kisses her hand).

Violetta—To-morrow—

Alfred—More I will ask not.
    (exit).

SCENE IV—VIOLETTA, and all the others, returning from the dancing-room.

All—In the east the dawn is breaking,
And perforce we must depart,
Gentle lady, leave now takinfi,
Thanks we give thee from each heart.
Full the city is of pleasure,
Brief the time for love and joy,
To repose give needful measure,
Lest enjoyment we destroy!
    (exeunt).

SCENE V—VIOLETTA, alone.

How wondrous! how wondrous! those accents
Upon my heart are graven!
Will it misfortune bring me, a love in earnest?
What shall be thy resolve, my troubled spirit?
No living man hath yet enflamed thee!
Oh, rapture that I have known not, to be loved and loving
Can my heart still disdain it
For follies dry and heartle s, which now enchain me?

Alfredo—Allor domani?

Violetta—Ebbene domani.

Alfredo—Io son felice!
    (prende còn trasporto il fiore.)

Violetta—D'amarmi dite ancora ?

Alfredo—Oh, quanto v'amo!
    (per partire.)

Violetta—Partite?

Alfredo—Parto.
    (torna a lei, e le bacia la mano.)

Violetta—Addio.

Alfredo—Di più non bramo.
    (Esce.)

SCENA IV—VIOLETTA e tutti gli altri che tornano dalla sala della danza.

Tutti—Si ridesta in ciel l' aurora,
E n' è forza ripartire;
Mercè a voi gentil Signora
    (a VIOLETTA.)
Di sì splendido gioir
La città di feste è piena,
Volge il tempo del piacer;
Nel riposo omai la lena
Si ritempri per goder.
    (Partono dalla destra.)

SCENA V—VIOLETTA sola.

E strano! è strano!—In core
Scolpiti ho quegli accenti!
Saria per mia sventura un serio amore?
Che risolvi, o turbata anima mia?
Null' uomo ancora t'accendeva.—Oh, gioia,
Ch'io non conobbi, esser amata amando!
E sdegnarla poss' io
Per l' aride follie del viver mio?

AH, FORS' E LUI — 'TWAS HE, PERLHANCE (Violetta)

Ah, fors' è lui che l'à-ni-ma so-lin-ga ne' tu-mul-ti,
Twas he, per-chance, my long-ing soul, Lone-ly, 'mid scenes of pleas-ure,

so-lin-ga ne' tu-mul-ti, go-dea so-ven-te pin-ge-re
lone-ly, 'mid scenes of pleas-ure, Oft loved to paint in col-ors bright,

de'suoi co-lo-ri oc-cul-ti, de'suoi co-lo-ri oc-cul-ti! Lui che, mo-des-to e
In its own gold and a-zure, In its own gold and a-zure, He, who with mod-est

vi - gi - le, all' e - gre sog - lie a - sce - se, e nuo - va fcb - bre ac - ce - se
ri - gi - lance, To my sick room re - turn-ing, Kin-dled new flames, still burn-ing,

des - tan - do - mi all' a - mor! A quell a - mor, quell' a - mor che e pal - pi - to dell' u - ni -
Des-tined my heart to love! Yes! this is love, 'tis the love that pal - pi-tates Through all the

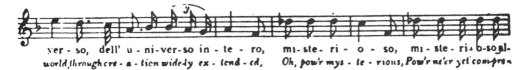

ver - so, dell' u - ni - ver - so in - te - ro, mi - ste - ri - o - so, mi - ste - ri o - so al -
world, through cre - a - tion wide-ly ex - tend - ed, Oh, pow'r mys - te - rious, Pow'r ne'er yet com pre -

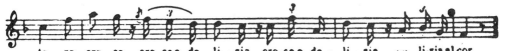

te - ro, cro - ce, cro - ce e de - li - zia, cro - ce e de - li - zia, de - li - zia al cor.
hend - ed. Tor - ment, tor - ment and rap - ture, tor - ment and rap - ture each do we prove.

To my young heart, all guileless then,
Filled with intrepid yearning,
This dream was imaged, fair, serene,
Bright o'er my pathway burning.
When like a star from heaven,
Radiant he stood before me,
Visions of hope came o'er me.
Like the found dreams I wove.
Then beat my heart with the love that
palpitates
Through all the world, thro' creation wide
extended.
Oh! pow'r mysterious, pow'r ne'er yet com-
prehended.
Torment and rapture, each do we prove.
(remains for an instant buried in thought, then says:)
What folly! All this is vain delirium!
Child of misfortune, lonely,
By all abandoned, in this gay croweded desert,
This vortex of pleasure they call Paris,
What hope remains? what must I do, then?
Surrender to pleasure's maddening whirl
again?

A me, fanciulla, un candido
E trepido desire
Quest' effigiò, dolcissimo
Signor dell' avvenire,
Quando ne' cieli il raggio
Di sua beltà vedea,
E tutta me pascea
Di quel soave error
Sentia che amore è palpito
Dell' universo intero,
Misterioso, altero,
Pena e delizia al cor.
(resta concentrata un istante poi dice.)
Follie! — follie! — delirio vano è questo!
In quai sogni mi perdo!
Povera donna, sola,
Abbandonata in questo popoloso
deserto,
Che appellano Parigi,
Che spero or più? — Che far degg' io? —
gioire.
Di voluttà nei vortici finire.

SEMPRE LIBERA — *EVER FREE, SHALL I STILL WANDER* (Voletta)

Sem - pro li - be - ra — degg' i - o fol - leg - gia - re di gio - ja in
Ev - er free, shall I — still wan - der Mad - ly on from pleas - ure to

gio - ja, vo' che scor - ra il vi - ver mi - o pei sen - tie - ri del pia -
pleas - ure? Life's short mo - ments shall — I squan - der In pur - suit of fol - lies

ccr? Nas-cail gior-no, oj l gior-no muo-ja sem-pre lie - ta ne' ri-.
gay? Days pass by me in rap-id meas-ure, Hap-piest where light hearts are.

tro - vi, _____ a di - let - ti sem - pre nuo - vi dee vo -
throng - ing, _____ For new pleas-ures ev - er long .. ing, Shall my

la - re il mio pen - sier, dee _____ vo - lar, dee _____ vo - lar, dee _____ vo -
thoughts fly i - dly a - way, fly _____ a - way, fly _____ a - way, Shall _____ my

la - re il mio pen - sier, dee _____ vo - lar, dee _____ vo
thoughts _____ fly i - dly a - way, fly _____ a - way, i - dly

lar _____ il pen - sier.
fly, _____ fly a - way

(exit on the left). | (parte, a sinistra.)
END OF THE FIRST ACT. | FINE DELL' ATTO PRIMO.

ACT II.

SCENE 1—A country house near Paris. A salon on the ground floor. At the back, facing the audience, a fireplace, over which is a looking glass A clock hangs between two glass doors, which are closed. There are also two side doors, seats, tables, and writing materials.

(ALFRED enters, in sporting costume)

Alfred—Out from her presence, for me there's no enjoyment.
(puts down his gun).
Three months have flown already
Since my beloved Violetta
So kindly left for me her riches, admirers,
And all the haunts of pleasure,
Where she had been accustomed
To hommage from all hearts, for charms transcendent,
Yet now contented in this retreat, so qquiet,
She forgets all for me. Here, near my loved one,
New life springs within me
From the trials of love restored and strengthened,
Ah! in my present rapture past sorrows are forgotten.

ATTO II.

SCENA I—Casa di Campagna presso Parigi. Saloto terreno. Nel fondo, in faccia agli Spettatori, è un camino, sopra il quale uno specchio ed un orologio, fra due porto chiuse da cristalli, che mettono ad un giardino. Al primo panno due altre porte, una di fronte all' altra. Sedie, tavolini, qualche libro, l'occorrente per scrivere.

(ALFREDO entra, in costume da caccia)

Alfredo—Lunge da lei per me non v' ha dilette!
(depone il fucile.)
Volaron già tre lune
Dacchè la mia Violetta
Agi per me lascio, dovizie, onori.
E le pompose feste,
Ove agli omaggi avvezza,
Vedea schiavo ciascun di sua bellezza—
E dal suffio d'amor rigenerato
Solo esiste per me—qui presso a lei
Io rinascer mi sento,
E dal suffio d'amor rigenerato
Scordo ne' gaudj suoi tutto il passato.

DI MIEI BOLLENTI SPIRITI—*ALL MY IMPULSIVE ECTASIES* (Alfred)

De miei bol-len spi - ri-ti il gio-va-ni le ar-do-re, el - la tem-prò col
All my im-pul-so ec-sta-sies, Spring from a youthful ar - dor, She hath subdued with

10

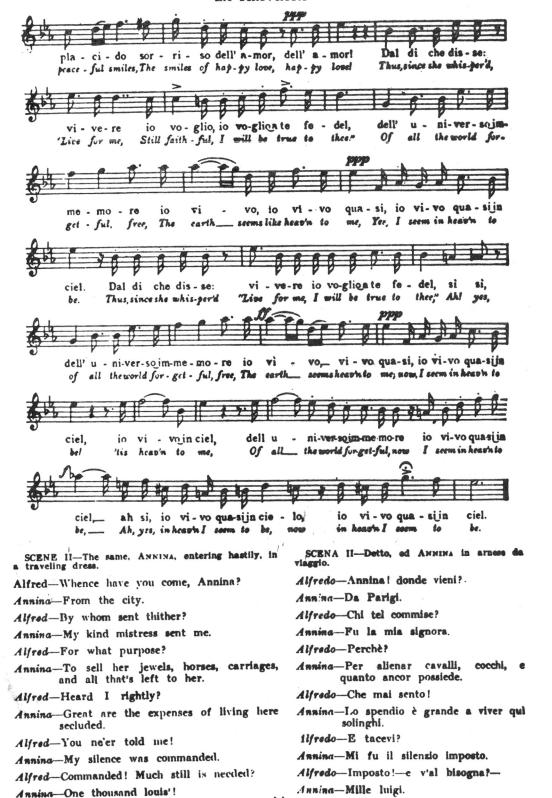

pla - ci - do sor - ri - so dell' a-mor, dell' a-mor! Dal di che dis-se:
peace - ful smiles, The smiles of hap-py love, hap-py love! Thus, since she whis-per'd,

vi - ve - re io vo - glio, io vo-glio a te fe - del, dell' u - ni-ver-so im-
'Live for me, Still faith-ful, I will be true to thee." Of all the world for-

me - mo - re io vi - vo, io vi - vo qua - si, io vi - vo qua - si in
get - ful, free, The earth____ seems like heav'n to me, Yet, I seem in heav'n to

ciel. Dal di che dis-se: vi - ve - re io vo-glio a te fe - del, si si,
be. Thus, since she whis-per'd "Live for me, I will be true to thee;" Ah! yes,

dell' u - ni-ver-so im-me-mo - re io vi - vo, vi - vo qua-si, io vi-vo qua-si in
of all the world for - get - ful, free, The earth____ seems heav'n to me; now, I seem in heav'n to

ciel, io vi - vo in ciel, dell u - ni-ver-so im-me-mo-re io vi-vo qua si in
be! 'tis heav'n to me, Of all____ the world for-get-ful, now I seem in heav'n to

ciel,___ ah si, io vi - vo qua-si in cie - lo, io vi-vo qua - si in ciel.
be, ____ Ah, yes, in heav'n I seem to be, now in heav'n I seem to be.

SCENE II—The same. ANNINA, entering hastily, in a traveling dress.

Alfred—Whence have you come, Annina?

Annina—From the city.

Alfred—By whom sent thither?

Annina—My kind mistress sent me.

Alfred—For what purpose?

Annina—To sell her jewels, horses, carriages, and all that's left to her.

Alfred—Heard I rightly?

Annina—Great are the expenses of living here secluded.

Alfred—You ne'er told me!

Annina—My silence was commanded.

Alfred—Commanded! Much still is needed?

Annina—One thousand louis'!

SCENA II—Detto, ed ANNINA in arnese da viaggio.

Alfredo—Annina! donde vieni?

Annina—Da Parigi.

Alfredo—Chi tel commise?

Annina—Fu la mia signora.

Alfredo—Perchè?

Annina—Per alienar cavalli, cocchi, e quanto ancor possiede.

Alfredo—Che mai sento!

Annina—Lo spendio è grande a viver qui solinghi.

Alfredo—E tacevi?

Annina—Mi fu il silenzio imposto.

Alfredo—Imposto!—e v'al bisogna?—

Annina—Mille luigi.

11

Alfred—Now leave me. I go to Paris.
  Mind that your mistress knows nothing of
    these questions.
  Ere long I shall be able to repair all. Go—
    go!

(ANNINA goes out).

SCENE III—ALFRED, alone.

Alfredo—Or vanne—Andrò a Parigi—
  Questo colluquio ignori la signora—
  Il tutto valgo a riparere ancora.

(ANNINA parte)

SCENA III—ALFREDO, solo.

O MIO RIMORSO!—*OH! DARK REMORSE!* (Alfred)

(departs).

(Esce.)

SCENE IV — VIOLETTA enters with papers in her
and; ANNINA, JOSEPH.

(to ANNINA).

Violetta—Alfred?

Annina—He has gone to Paris, madame.

Violetta—When to return?

Annina—Before the day is ended,
  He bade me tell you.

SCENA IV—VIOLETTA, ch'entra con alcune
carte, parlando, con ANNINA, poi GIUSEPPE a
tempo.

Violetta—Alfredo!

Annina—Per Parigi or or pàrtiva.

Violetta—E tornerà?

Annina—Pria che tramonti il giorno—dirvel
  m'impose.

12

Violetta—'Tis strang, this!
    (presents a letter).

Joseph—For you.

Violetta—'Tis well. A business agent shortly
    will arrive here;
At once admit him.
    (exeunt ANNINA and JOSEPH).

SCENE V — VIOLETTA, afterwards GERMONT, introduced by JOSEPH, who places two chairs, and goes out.

    (reading the letter.)

Violetta—Ah! ah!
So Flora hath my home discovered,
And invites me to join a dance this evening!
She'll look for me in vain!
    (Throws the letter on a table and seats herself).

Joseph—A man would see you.

Violetta—'Tis the one I look'd for.
    (bids JOSEPH show him in).

Germont—Are you the lady of the house?

Violetta—I am, sir.

Germont—In me behold Alfred's father.

Violetta—You?
    (with surprise, invites him to be seated).

Germont—Yes, of the imprudent, who goes fast
    to ruin,
Led away by your follies.
    (rising, resentfully).

Violetta—Stay, sir, I am a lady in my own
    dwelling,
And perforce I must leav you, for your
    sake more than mine.
    (about to retire).

Germont—(What manners!) But then—

Violetta—You have been led in error.
    (returns to her seat).

Germont—He will spend all his fortune upon you.

Violetta—He has not yet offered. I should refuse.

Germont—How then such grandeur?
    (looking around).

Violetta—This deed is to all else a mystery—
    to you 'twill not be.
    (gives him a paper).
    (reads the paper).

Germont—Heav'n, what a statement!
Have you then determined all your wealth
    to dispose of?
But, your past life, ah, why must that
    accuse you?

Violetta—It does so no longer; Alfred I love
    now, and Heav'n
Has cancell'd all the past with my repentance.

Germont—Ah, you have noble feelings.

Violetta—Like sweet music my ear receives your
    accents.
    (rising).

Germont—And of such feelings a sacrifice I
    ask now.
    (rising).

Violetta—E strano!
    (la presenta una lettera.)

Giuseppe—Per voi.
    (la prende.)

Violetta—Sta bene. In breve
Giungerà un uom d' affari—entri all'
    istante.
    (ANNINA e GIUSEPPE escono.)

SCENA V—VIOLETTA, quindi il Sig. GERMONT, introdotto da GIUSEPPE, che, avanza due siede, e parte.

    (leggendo la lettera.)

Violetta—Ah, ah,
Scuopriva Flora il mio ritiro!—
E m'invita a danzar per questa sera!
In van m'aspetterà.
    (Getta il foglio sul tavolino e siede.)

Giuseppe—Giunse un signore.

Violetta—Ah! sarà lui che attendo.
    (Accenna a GIUSEPPE d'introd.)

Germont—Madamigella Valery?

Violetta—Son io.

Germont—D' Alfredo il padre in me vedete.

Violetta—Voi!
    (Sorpresa gli accenna di sedere.)

Germont—Sì, dell' incanto, che a rovina
    corre,
Ammaliato da voi.
    (Sedendo.)

Violetta—Donna son io, signore, ed in mia
    (alzandosi risentita.)
    casa;
Ch'io vi lasci assentite,
Più per voi, che per me.
    (per uscire.)

Germont—(Quai modi!) Pure—

Violetta—Tratto in error voi foste.
    (torna a sedere.)

Germont—De' suoi beni donovuol farvi.

Violetta—Non l' oso finora.—Rifiuterei.

Germont—Pur tanto lusso—
    (gli da le carte.)

Violetta—A tutti è mistero quest' atto.—
A voi nol sia

    (dopo averle scorse coll' occhic.)

Germont—D'ogni avere pensate dispogliarvi!—
Ah, il passato perchè, perchè v'accusa!

Violetta—Più non esiste—or amo Alfredo,
    e Dio
Lo cancellò col pentimento mio.

Germont—Nobile sensi invero!

Violetta—Oh, come dolce mi suona il
    vostra accento!

Germont—Ed a tai sensi un sacrifizio
    chieggo.

Violetta—Ah, no, pray do not!
A dreadful thing thou wouldst require, I'm certain.
I foresaw it, with terror; ah, I was far too happy!

Germont—A father's honor requires it,
And the future of his two dear children claims it.

Violetta—Of two children?

Germont—Yes.

Violetta—Ah, no, tacete—
(alzandosi.)
Terribil cosa chiedereste, certo—
Il predevi, v'attesi, era felice troppo.

Germont—D'Alfredo il padre la sorte,
L'avvenir domanda or qui de' suoi due figli.

Violetta—Di due figli?

Germont—Sì.

PURA SICCOME—*PURE AS AN ANGEL* (Germont)

Pu - ra sic - co - me un an - ge - lo
Pure as an an - gel from a - bove,
Id - dio mi diè u - na fi - glia,
Kind heav'n a daugh-ter gave me,

se Al - fre - do nie - ga rie - de - re in se - no al - la fa - mi - glia,
If now Al - fre - do to our love Will not re - turn and save me;

l'a - ma - to e a - man - te gio - vi - ne, cui spo - sa an - dar do -
He, the be - lov'd and lov - ing youth, Who soon should wed my

ve - a, or si ri - cu - sa al vin - co - lo__ che__
daugh - ter, Must then with - draw his plight - ed troth, With

lie - ti, lie - ti ne ren - de - va. Deh non mu - ta - te jn tri - bo - li
all the joy, the joy it brought her. Then do not change love's ro - ses fair

le ro - se dell' a - mor, ah, non mu - ta - te jn tri - bo - li le ro - se dell' a -
To thorns of grief and pain, Ah, do not change love's ro - ses fair To thorns of grief and

mor a' prie - ghi miei re - sis - te - re no, no, non vo - glia il vos-tro cor, no, no.
pain, Your gen-'rous heart, to my fond prayr, no, no, Will not op-posed re-main, no, no.

Violetta—Ah! I Isee now, that I must for a season
Be from Alfred parted. 'Twill be painful,
Dreary for me, yet—

Germont—That will not suffice me!

Violetta—Heav'ns! What more dost seek for?
Enough I've offered!

Violetta—Ah, comprendo—dovrò per alcun tempo
Da Alfredo allontanarmi—doloroso
Fora per me—pur—

Germont—Non è ciò che chiedo.

Violetta—Cielo!—che più cercate?—offersi assai!

Germont—No, not quite yet.

Violetta—You wish that I forever renounce him?

Germont—It must be.

Violetta—Ah, no! I cannot—never!
Ah! thou know'st not what affection
Burns within me, ardent, living!
Not one kind friend or connexion
Can I number, still surviving?
But Alfred has declared it,
All in him my heart should find!
Ah! thou know'st not what dark sorrow
Mocked my being with its shadow?
All is over—how sad the morrow,
Parted thus from dear Alfred!
Ah! the trial is too cruel;
It' were better far to die.

Germont—The sacrifice is heavy;
But hear me with tranquility.
Lovely thou art still, and youthful, too
Hereafter—

Violetta—No more persuade me. I know all,
But it cannot be. Him only I love and
live for!

Germont—So be it. But the men are oft unfaithful still—
(astounded).

Violetta—Great Heaven!

Germont—Some day, when love hath colder grown,
And time's broad gulf yawns wider;
When all the joys of life have flown,
What then will be? Consider!
No healing balm shall soothe your rest,
No warm and deep affection,
Since Heav'n your ties will ne'er have blest
with holy benediction.

Violetta—'Tis all true!

Germont—Then haste to dissipate the spell
Of this bright dream, controlling;
Be to my home and loved ones
Our angel, good, consoling.
Violetta, oh, consider well
While yet there may be time.
'Tis Heav'n itself that bids me speak,
'Tis Heav'n inspiring
These words in faith sublime.

Violetta—Thus, to the wretched, who falls, frail and erring,
When once again she would rise, hope is silent.
Though Heaven's indulgent, its pardon conferring,
Man unforgiving to her will be.
Say to this child of thine, young, pure and lovely,
Thou has a victim found, whose life of sadness
Had but one single ray of rapture and gladness
Which she will yield to her, then gladly die.

Germont—Pur non basta.

Violetta—Volete che per sempre a lui renunzi?

Germont—E d'uopo.

Violetta—Ah, no—giam no, mai!
Non sapete quale affetto
Vivo, immenso in' arda il petto?
Che nè amici, nè parenti
Io non conto tra' viventi?
E che Alfredo m' ha giurato
Che in lui tutto io troverò?
Non sapete che colpita
D'atro murbo è la mia vita?
Che già presso il fin ne vedo?
Ch'io mi separi da Alfredo!
Ah, il supplizio è si spietato,
Che morir preferiro.

Germont—E grave il sacrifizio,
Ma pur, tranquilla udite.
Bella voi siete e giovane—
Col tempo—

Violetta—Ah, più non dite—v'intendo—
M' è impossible—Lui solo amar vogl'io.

Germont—Sia pure—ma volubile sovente è l'uom.
(colpita.)

Violetta—Gran Dio!

Germont—Un di, quando le veneri
Il tempo avrà fugate,
Fia presto il tedic a sorgere—
Che sarà allor!—pensate—
Per voi non avran balsamo
I più soavi affetti!
Da un genitor non furono
Tai nodi benedetti.

Violetta—E vero!

Germont—Ah, dunque, sperdasi
Tal sogno seduttore—
Siate di mia famiglia
L'angiol consolatore—
Violetta, deh pensateci,
Ne siete in tempo ancor.
E Dio che inspira, o giovana,
Tai detti a un genitor.

Violetta—Cosi alla misera, ch' è un di caduta,
Di più risorgere speranza e' muta!
Se pur benefico le indulga Iddio
L'uomo implacabile per lei sarà.
Dite alla giovine si bella e pura,
Ch'avvi una vittima, della sventure
Cui resta un unico raggio di bene
Che a lei il sagrifica e che morrà.

Germont—Weep on, thou hapless one,
Weep on; I witness thy trial
In what I ask of thy selfdenial.
Bear up, thou noble heart, triump is nigh.

Violetta—Now command me.

Germont—Tell him that thou lovest him not.

Violetta—He'll not believe.

Germont—Then leave him.

Violetta—He'll follow.

Germont—Well, then—

Violetta—Embrace me as thy daughter, then
will my heart be strong.
Ere long, restored you'll find him; but sad
(they embrace).
beyond all telling.
Then, to console him, from the arbor approach him.
(points to the garden and sits down to write).

Germont—What art thinking?

Violetta—If you my thoughts could know, you
would then oppose me.

Germont—Generous-hearted! How can I e'er
repay thee?

Violetta—I shall die! let not my memory
By him be execrated,
But let my woes and trials dark
To him be all related.
This sacrifice o'erwhelming
I make of love to duty,
Will be the end of all my woe,
The last sigh of my heart.

Germont—No, noble heart, thou still shalt live!
A bright fate shall redress thee;
These tears anounce the happy day
That Heav'n will send to bless thee.
This sacrifice unbounded
You make of love to duty,
So noble is, 'twill soon a glow
Of pride to you impart

Violetta—Some one comes, retire now.

Germont—Oh, how my heart is grateful!

Violetta—We meet no more forever!
(they embrace.)

Both—May you be happy—Heav'n bless thee!
(GERMONT goes out by the garden door).

SCENE VI—VIOLETTA, then ANNINA, then ALFRED.

Violetta—Oh, grant me strength, kind Heaven!
(sits down, writes, and then rings the bell).

Annina—Do you require me?

Violetta—Yes; take and deliver thou this letter.
(looks at the direction with surprise).

Annina—Oh!

Violetta—Be silent; go directly.
(exit ANNINA).
I must write to him now. What shall I say?
Where shall I find the courage?
(writes, then seals the letter).

Germont—Piangi, piangi, o misera,
Supremo il veggo è il sagrifizio
Ch'orati chieggo.
Sento nell' anima già le tue pene
Coraggio, è il nobile cor vincerà.

Violetta—Imponete.

Germont—Non amarlo ditegli.

Violetta—Nol crederà.

Germont—Partite.

Violetta—Seguirammi.

Germont—Allor.

Violetta—Qual figlia m'abbraciate—forte
cosi saro.
(S'abbracciano.)
Tra breve ei vi fia reso, ma afflitto
oltare ogni dire;
A suo conforto di colà volerete.
(Indicandogli il giardino, va ver iscrivere.)

Germont—O che pensate!

Violetta—Sapendo, v' opporreste al pensier
mio.

Germont—Generosa!—e per voi che far
poss' io?

Violetta—Morrò—la mia memoria;
(tornando a lui.)
Non fia ch' ei maledica,
Se le mie pene orribili
Vi sia chi almen gli dica.
Conosca il sacrifizio
Ch' io consumai d'amor.
Che sarà suo fin l'ultimo
Sospiro del mio cor.

Germont—No generosa, vivere,
E lieto voi dovrete,
Mercè di queste lagrime
Dal cielo un giorno avrete,
Premiato il sacrifizio
Sarà del vostro cor.
D'un' opra così nobile
Andrete fiera allor.

Violetta—Qui giunge alcun; partite!

Germont—Ah, grato v' è il cor mio!

Violetta—Non ci vedrem più, forse.
(S'abbracciano.)

A due—Felice siate—Addio!

SCENA VI — VIOLETTA, poi ANNINA, guindi ALFREDO.
(GERMONT esce la porta del giardino.)

Violetta—Dammi tu forza, o cielo!
(siede, scrive, poi suona il campanelle.)

Annina—Mi chiedeste?

Violetta—Sì, reca tu stessa questa foglio.
(ne guarda la direzione, a se na mestru sorpresa.)

Annina—Oh!

Violetta—Silenzio—va all'istante.
(ANNINA parte.)
Ed or si scriva a lui—che gli dire?
Chi men darà il coraggio?
(scrive e poi suggella.)

Alfred—What now?   (coming in).

Violetta—Nothing.   (conceals the letter).

Alfred—Wert writing?

Violetta—Yes—no—

Alfred—What strange confusion! To whom wert writing?

Violetta—To thee.

Alfred—Give me the letter.

Violetta—No—directly.

Alfred—Forgive me; my thoughts are quite disturbed.   (rising).

Violetta—By what?

Alfred—News from my father.

Violetta—Hast seen him?

Alfred—Ah no! but he hath sent a cruel letter! I soon expect him. At a glance he will love thee.   (with agitation).

Violetta—Let him not here surprise me.
Allow me to retire now, thou wilt calm him;
Then at his feet—I'll humbly fall—
    (scarcely restraining her tears).
He cannot will that we should part—we shall be happy—
Because thou lov'st me, Alfred—is it not so?

Alfred—Oh, dearly! why dost weep thus?

Violetta—My heart, o'ercharged, had need of weeping—I now am tranquil,
Thou seest it?—Smiling on thee!
    (with great effort).
I'll be there—'mid the flow'rs, ever near thee,—
Love me Alfred, love me as I now love thee.
Farewell, love!
    (Runs to the garden.)

SCENE VII—ALFRED, then JOSEPH, then a MESSENGER.

Alfred—Ah, that fond heart lives only in my devotion!
(sits down and opens a book, reads a little, then rises, and looks at the clock, which is upon the chimneypiece).
'Tis late now! to-day it's doubtful
I shall see my father.

    (enters hurriedly).

Joseph—Sir, my lady has departed,
In a carriage that awaited,
And is already upon the road to Paris.
Annina, too, disappeared some time before her.

Alfred—I know—be quiet.

Joseph—(What does this mean?)
    (retires).

Alfred—She goes, perhaps, to hasten
The sale of all her property.
Annina will stay all that.
(His father is seen in the distance, crossing the garden).
Someone is in the garden!
Who's there?

    (going out meets messenger at door)

Messenger—You, sir, are Germont?

Alfredo—Che fai?

Violetta—Nulla.   (nascendendo la lettera.)

Alfredo—Scrivevi?

Violetta—No—sì—   (confusa.)

Alfredo—Qual turbamento?—a chi scrivevi?

Violetta—A te.

Alfredo—Dammi quel foglio.

Violetta—No, per ora.

Alfredo—Mi perdona—son io preoccupato.
    (alzandosi.)

Violetta—Che fu?

Alfredo—Giunse mio padre.

Violetta—Lo vedesti?

Alfredo—Ah, no; un severo scritto mi lasciava—
Ma verrà—t'amerà solo in vederti.

Violetta—Ch'io qui non mi sorprenda—
    (molto agitata.)
Lascia che m'allontani—tu lo calma—
Ai piedi suoi mi getterò—divisi
    (mal frenando il pianto.)
Ei più non è vorrà--sarem felici—
Perchè tu m'ami, Alfredo, non è vero?

Alfredo—Oh, quanto!—perchè piangi?

Violetta—Di lagrime avea duopo—or son tranquilla—
Lo vedi?—ti sorrido—
    (forzandosi.)
Sarò là, tra quei fior, presso a te sempre—
Amami, Alfredo, quant' io t'amo.—Addio.
    (corre in giardino.)

SCENA VII—ALFREDO, poi GIUSEPPE, indi un COMMISSIONARO, a tempo.

Alfredo—Ah, vive sol quel core all' amor mio!
(Siede, prende a caso un libro, legge alquanto, quando s'alza, guarda l'ora sull' orologio sovroposto al camino.)
E tardi; ed oggi forse.
Più non verrà mio padre.
    (Entrando frettoloso.)

Giuseppa—La signora è partita—
L' attendeva un calesse, e sulla via
Già corre di Parigi.—Annina pure
Prima di lei spariva.

Alfredo—Il sò, ti calma.
    (da se.)

Giuseppe—Che vuol dir ciò!
    (Esce.)

Alfredo—Va forse d' ogni avere
Ad affrettar la perdita—
Ma Annina la impedirà.
(Si vede il Padre attraversare in lontane il giardino.)
Qualcuno è nel giardino!
Chi è là?
    (per uscire.)
    (alla porta.)

Commissionaro—Il Signor Germont?

Alfred—I am, sir.

Messeng.—Sir, a lady in a coach, gave me,
Not far from this place, a note, to you
directed.

(gives a letter to ALFRED, is paid and departs).

SCENE VIIII — ALFRED, then GERMONT, from the garden.

Alfred—From Violetta! ah, why am I thus moved?
To rejoin her, perhaps she now invites me.
I tremble.
Oh, Heav'n! send courage!
(opens and reads).
"Alfred, at the moment this note shall reach
you"—
Ah!

[He utters a cry like one struck by a thunderbolt, and in turning finds himself in the presence of his father, into whose arms he throws himself, exclaiming:)
Oh, my father!

Germont—My dear son!
How thou dost suffer! restrain thy weeping,
Return and be the glory, the pride of thy
father.

(ALFRED despairingly sits at a table, with his face concealed in his hands).

Alfredo—Son io.

Commissionaro—Una dama, da un cocchio,
per voi,
Di quà non lunge mi diede questo
scritto.
(Da una lettera ad ALFREDO, ne riceve qualche moneta, e parte.)

SCENA VIII—ALFREDO, poi GERMONT, ch'entra dal giardino.

Alfredo—Di Violetta! — Perchè son io
commosso?—
A raggiungerla forse ella m' invita—
Io tremo!—Oh ciel!—Coraggio!
(apre e legge.)
"Alfredo, al giungervi di questo foglio
(come fulminato, grida.)
(Volgendosi, si trova a fronte del padre, nelle cui braccia si abbandona, esclamando:)
Ah!—Padre mio!

Germont.—Mio figlio!
Oh, quanto soffri—tergi, ah, tergi il
pianto—
Ritorna di tuo padre orgolio e vanto.
(ALFREDO disperato siede presso il tavolino col volte tra le mani.)

DI PROVENZA IL MAR—*FROM FAIR PROVENCE'S SOIL AND SEA* (Germont)

Di Pro - ven-za il mar il suol chi dal cor-ti can-cel-lò? chi dal
From fair Pro-vence soil and sea, Who hath won thy heart a - way, Who hath

cor-ti can-cel-lò? di Pro-ven-za il mar il suol? al na-tio ful-gen-te sol qual de-
won thy heart a-way, From fair Pro-vence soil and sea? From thy na-tive sunny clime, What strange

sti-no ti fu-rò? qual de-sti-no ti fu-rò? al na-tio ful-gen-te sol? Oh, ram-
fate caused thee to stray, What strange fate caused thee to stray From thy na-tive sun-ny clime? Oh, re-

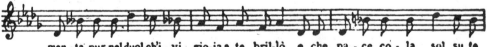

men-ta pur nel duol ch'i-vi gio-ja a te bril-lò, e che pa-ce co-la sol su te
mem-ber in thy woe All the joy that waits for thee, All the peace thy heart would know, On-ly

splen-de-re an-cor può, e che pa-ce co-la sol su te splen-de-re an-cor può.
there still found may be. All the peace thy heart would know, On-ly there, still found may be.

Dio mi gui-dò! Dio mi gui-dò! Dio mi gui dò!
Heav'n guid-ed me! Heav'n guid-ed me! Heav'n guid-ed me!

Ah, thy father old and worn,
  What he felt, thou ne'er canst know.
IIn thine absence, so forlorn
  Seemed his home, with grief and woe.
But I find thee now again,
  If my hope doth not mislead,
  With its voice not mute or dead,
Heav'n sends me aid!
Wilt not answer a father's affection?

(embracing him).

Alfred—Countless furies within my heart are raging!
  Go and leave me—
    (repulses his father).

Germont—How, leave thee?

Alfred—(Oh, for vengeance!)

Germont—Do not linger, let's go now, oh, haste thee!

Alfred—(It was Dauphol!)

Germont—Dost thou not hear?

Alfred—No!

Germont—All in vain then my search will have been?
  No, no, I will not chide thee now,
  But hide the past forever;
  The love that guides me ever
  Full pardon will bestow.
  Then come and drown thy care in joy
  With me again returning;
  For thee loved ones are yearning;
  Such hopes thou'lt not destroy!
  Fond hearts at home are burning
  Their soothing care to show.

(arousing himself; sees upon the table the letter of FLORA, glances at its contents, and exclaims:)
Alfred—Ah' She's at the fete, then!
  Thither will I fly, and seek revenge.

Germont—What say'st thou? ah, stay thee!

(ALFRED departs precipitately, followed by his father).

SCENE IX—A salon in FLORA's palace, richly furnished and lighted up. A door in the back scene, and two lateral ones On the right, a little forward, a table, on which are cards and other implements of play. On the left a small table, with flowers and refreshments; chairs and a settee.
(FLORA, the MARQUIS, the DOCTOR, and other guests, enter from the left, and converse amongst themselves).

Flora—There'll be fun here to-night with maskers merry;
  The Count will be their leader;
  Violetta and Alfred both will be here.

Marquis—Have you not heard the news then?
  Germont and Violetta are divided.

Doctor
Flora } Is that true?

Marquis—Yes, and she will come with the Baron.

Doctor—I saw them yesterday, appearing quite happy.
    (a noise is heard on the right).
Flora—Be silent—you hear them?

All—Yes, our friends are coming.

Oh! il tuo vecchio genitor
  Tu non sai quanto soffri—
Te lontano, di squallor
  Il suo tetto si copri—
Ma se alfin ti trovo ancor
  Se in me speme non falli.
Se la voce dell' onor
  In te appien non ammuti—
Dio m'esaudi!
Nè rispondi d'un padre all'affeto.

(abbracciando.)

Alfredo—Mille furie divorammi il petto—
  Mi lasciate—

(respingendolo.)

Germont—Lasciarti!

Alfredo—(Oh, vendetta!)
    (risoluto.)
Germont—Non più indugi; partiamo—t'affretta.

Alfredo—(Ah, fu Douphol!)

Germont—M'ascolti tu?

Alfredo—No!

Germont—Dunque invano trovoato t'avrò!
  No, non udrai rimproveri;
  Copriam d'oblio il passato;
  L'amor che m'ha guidato
  Sa tutto perdonar.
  Vieni, i tuoi cari in giubilo
  Con me rivedi ancora;
  A chi penò finora
  Tal gioja non mlegar
  Un padre ed una suora
  T'affretta a consolar.

(Scuotendosi, getta a caso gli occhi sulla tavola, a vede la lettera di FLORA, la scorre ed esclama:)
Alfredo—Ah!—ell' è alla festa!—volisi
  L' offesa a vendicar.

Germont—Che dice? ah ferma!

(fugge precipitoso seguito dal padre.)

SCENA IX—Galleria nel palazzo di FLORA, riccamente addobata ed illuminata. Una porta nel fondo e due laterali. A destra più avanti un tavoliere con quanto occorre pel giuoco; a sinistra, ricco tavolino con fiori e rinfreschi, varie sedis e un divano.
(FLORA, il MARCHESE, il DOTTORE, ed altri invitati entrano dalla sinistra, discorrendo tra loro.)

Flora—Avrem lieta di maschere la notte;
  N' è duce il viscontino—
  Violetta ed Alfredo anco invitai.

Marchese—La Novita ignorate?
  Violetta e Germont son disgiunti.

Dottore
Flora } Fia vero.

Marchese—Ella verrà qui col barone.

Dottore—Li vidi jeri ancor—Parean felici.
    (S' ode rumore a destra)

Flora—Silenzio—Udite?
    (vanno verso la destra.)
Tutti—Giungono gli amici.

SCENE X—The same, and a number of ladies masked as Gipsies, some of whom hold a staff in the hand, same have tambourines, with which to beat time.

SCENA X—Detti, e molte Signore mascherate da Zingare, che entrano dalla destra.

NOI SIAMO ZINGARELLE—*WE'RE GIPSIES GAY AND YOUTHFUL* (Chorus)

Allegro moderato

Noi sia - mo zin - ga - rel - le ve - nu - te da lon - ta - no: d'o-
We're gip - sies gay and youth - ful, From dis - tant shores ar - riv - ing: With

gau - no sul - la ma - no leg - gia - mo l'av - ve - nir, Se __
skil - ful art con - triv - ing The fu - ture to fore - tell, We __

con - sul - tiam le stel - le, con - sul - tiam le stel - le null' av - vi a noi d'os - cu - ro no, null'
read the plan - ets truth - ful, read the plan - ets truth - ful, Their se - crets dark un - fold - ing, all their

av - vi a noi d'os - cu - ro, e i ca - si del fu - tu - ro pos - sia - mo al - trui pre -
se - crets dark un - fold, The realms of fate be - hold - ing, We can your for - tunes

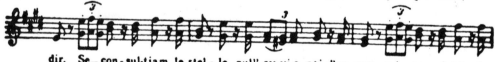

dir. Se - con - sul - tiam le stel - le null' av - vi a noi d'os - cur, e i ca - si del fu -
tell. We read the plan - ets truth - ful, Their se - crets dark un - fold, The realms of fate be -

tu - ro pos - sia - mo al - trui pre - dir, e i ca - si del fu - tu - ro, e i ca - si del fu -
hold - ing, We can your for - tunes tell, The realms of fate be - hold - ing, We can thus your fortunes

tur e - i ca - si del fu - tu - ro pos - sia - mo al - trui, pos - sia - mo al - trui pre -
tell, All the realms of fate be - hold - ing, we thus can tell, For - tunes we thus can

dir e - i ca - si del fu - tu ro, e - i ca - si del fu - tur, e - i ca - si del fu -
tell, All the realms of fate be - hold - ing, We can thus your for - tunes tell, All the realms of fate be -

tu - ro pos - sia - mo al - trui, pos - sia - mo al - trui pre - dir.
hold - ing, We thus can tell, for - tunes we thus can tell.

(examining the hand of FLORA).

First Gipsy—Let's see now. You, fair lady,
Have rivals gay and sprightly.

(examining the hand of the MARQUIS).

Second Gipsy—And you, if we read rightly,
As not the type of truth.

(to the MARQUIS).

Flora—You play me false already?
I'll take good care to pay you.

(to FLORA)

Marqquis—Ah, what the deuce thus say you?
The charge is base untruth.

Flora—The fox, howe'er disguising
Will yet be low and vicious;
Gay Marquis, be judicious,
Or else you may repent.

All—Let now a veil oblivious
Be o'er the past extended;
What's done may not be mended,
But future wrongs prevent.

(FLORA and the MARQUIS shake hands).

SCENE XI—The same; GASTON and others, masked
as Spanish Mattadores, and others as Piccadores, who
enter in a lively manner from the right.

Gaston and Tenors—We are Mattadores from
Madrid, so famous;
Bold and valiant in Bull-fights all name us;
Just arrived here, to join with discretion
In the fun of the "Fat ox" procession.
If a tale may command your attention,
You will find us gallants of pretention.

All the Others—Yes, yes, bravi! go on now re-
lating.
With much pleasure we'll listen.

Gaston and Chorus—Hear then.

1. *Zingara*—Vediamo?—Voi, signora,
(prendono la mano a FLORA, e la osservano.)
Rivali alquante avete.

2. *Zingara*—Márchese, voi non siete
Model di fedeltà.
(fanno lo stesso al MARCHESE.)

Flora—Fate il galante ancora?
Ben vo' me la paghiate.

(al MARCHESE.)
(a FLORA.)

Marchese—Che diacin vi pensate?
L' accusa è falsità.

Flora—Va volpe lascia il pelo,
Non abbandona il vizio;
Marchese mio, giudizio—
O vi farò pentir.

Tutti—Su via, si stenda unvelo
Sui fatti del passato;
Già quel ch' è stato è stato,
Badiano al l'avvenir.

(FLORA ed il MARCHESE si stringono la mano.)

SCENA XI—Detti, GASTONE ed altri maschrati
di Mattadori e Piccadori spagnuoli, ch'entrano
vivacemente dalla destra.

Gastone e Mattadori....Di Madride noi siam
mattadori,
Siamo i prodi del circo de' tori;
Testè giunti a godere del chiasso
Che a Parigi si fa pel Bue grasso;
E una storia se udire vorrete,
Qualti amanti noi siamo, saprete.

Gli Altri—Sì, sì, bravi; nárrate, narrate;
Con piacere l' udremo.

Gastone e Mattadori—Ascoltate.

E PIQUILLO UN BEL GAGLIARDO—YOUNG PIQUILLO (Gaston and Chorus)

E____ Pi-quil-lo un bel____ ga-gliar-do bi-sca-gli-no mat-ta-dor,
Young Pi-quil-lo, gay____ and dar-ing, Was____ a val-iant mat-ta-dor,

for-te il brac-cio, fie-ro il guar-do, del-le gio-stre e-gli è sig-nor.
Strong his arm was, proud his bear-ing, In____ all sports, the prize he bore.

D'An-da-lu-sia gio-vi-net-ta fol-le-men-te in-na-mo-rò;
One____ of Spain's fair maids en-chant-ing, With this youth fell mad-ly in love:

ma-la bel-la ri-tro-set-ta co-si al gio-va-ne____ par-lò:
But____ the maid, ere fa-vors grant-i-g, Bade him thus his val-or prove—

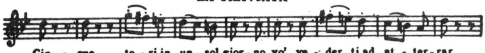

Cia - que to - ri in un sol gior - no vo' ve - der_ti ad at - ter - rar,
"Five stout bulls, in one brief morn-ing I would see_thee meet and slay;

e se vin - ci, al tuo ri - tor - no ma - no e cor_ ti vo' _ do-nar.
If suc - cess - ful, here re - turn-ing, Hand and heart shall thee re - pay."

Si_ gli dis-se e il mat - ta - do - ro al - le gio - stre mos - se il piè;
Then the mat - ta - dor_ as-sent-ed, To_ the tri - al led_ the way;

cin - que to - ri, vin - ci - to - re sull' a - re - na e - gli sten-dè;
Five fierce bulls, in turn pre-sent-ed, His strong arm did van-quish that day,

cin - que to - ri vin - ci - to - re sull' a - re - na e - gli sten - dè.
Five fierce bulls, in turn pre-sent - ed, His strong arm did van-quish that day.

Gli Altri.

Flora and Others—Bravely he with courage daring
Did his gallantry display!
While his love, with strength unsparing,
He declared in such gallant way.

Gaston and Chorus—Then, 'mid plaudits loud, returning
To the maid, with winning grace,
Took the prize with blushes burning,
Held her fast in love's embrace.

Others of the Chorus—Proofs we Mattadores thus render,
How we can vanquish all the fair!

Gaston—Here, the hearts are far more tender;
We content with trifling are.

All—Yes, let's try now to discover
All the various moods of fate;
The arena we uncover,
And for all bold players wait!

(The men take off their masks—some walk about, while others commence playing).

SCENE XII—The same, and ALFRED; then VIOLETTA with the BARON; afterwards, a servant.

All—Alfred!—you!

Alfred—Yes, my kind friends.

Flora—Violetta?

Alfred—I don't know.

All—What cool indifference! Bravo! We'll now commence to play.

Gli Altri—Bravo invero il mattadore
Ben gagliardo si mostrò,
Se alla giovine l' amore
In tal guisa egli provò.

Gastone e Mattadori—Poi, tra plausi, ritornato
Alla bella del suo cor,
Colse il premio desiato
Dal a fede, dall' amor.

Gli Altri—Con tai prove i mattadori
San le amanti conquistar!

Gastone e Mattadori—Ma diù sen più miti i cori;
A noi basta folleggiar.

Tutti—Sì, sì allegri—Or pria tentiamo
Della sorte il vario umor.
La palestra dischiudiamo
Agli audaci giuocator.

(Gli uomini si tolgono la maschera, chi passeggia e chi si accinge a giuocare.)

SCENA XII—Detti, ed ALFREDO, quindi VIOLETTA col BARONE; un Servo a tempo.

Tutti—Alfredo!—Voi!

Alfredo—Sì, amici.

Flora—Violetta?

Alfredo—Non ne so.

Tutti—Ben disinvolto!—Bravo!—Or via, giuocar
Si può

22

(GASTON shuffles the cards, ALFRED and others put up their stakes. VIOLETTA enters, leaning on the arm of the BARON).

Flora—Here comes the guest most welcome.

Violetta—To your kind wish I yielded.

Flora—Thanks to you, also, Baron, for your polite acceptance.
(softly to VIOLETTA).

Baron—Germont is here! do you see him?

Violetta—(Heav'n! 'tis he, truly!) I see him.

Baron—Let not one word escape you, addressed to this Alfred!

Violetta—(Why, ah, why came I hither? In mercy, Heaven, thy pity send to me!)

Flora—Sit here beside me. Tell me now, what new and strange is passing.

(To VIOLETTA, making her sit beside her on the settee. The DOCTOR approaches them while they are conversing in an undertone. The MARQUIS converses with the BARON. GASTON continues to play. ALFRED and others stake, and the rest walk about).

Alfred—A four-spot!

Gaston—Ah! thou hast wont it.

Alfred—Unfortunate in loving, makes fortunate in gaming—
(stakes again and wins).

All—Still he remains the victor.

Alfred—Oh I shall gain this evening, and with my golden winnings,
To the green fields returning, I shall again be happy.

Flora—Singly?

Alfred—No, no. With someone like her who once was with me, but fled and left me!

Violetta—(Oh, Heaven!)
(to ALFRED, pointing to VIOLETTA).

Gaston—Some pity show.
(with ill-restrained anger).

Baron—Beware!
(softly to the BARON).

Violetta—Be calm, or I must leave you.
(carelessly)

Alfred—Did you address me, Baron?
(ironically).

Baron—You are in such good fortune
I fain would try against you.

Alfred—Yes? I accept your challenge.

Violetta—(Who'll aid me? Death seems approaching.
Oh Heaven, look down and pity me!)
(staking).

Baron—Here at the right one hundred.
(staking).

Alfred—I, at the left one hundred.
(dealing off).

Gaston—An ace there, a knave, too; thou'st won it!

(GASTONE si pone a tagliare; ALFREDO ed altri puntano. VIOLETTA entra al braccio del BARONE.)
(andandole incontro.)

Flora—Qui desiata giungi.

Violetta—Cessi al cortese invito.

Flora—Grata vi son, Barone, d' averlo pur gradito.
(piano a VIOLETTA.)

Barone—Germont è qui! il vedete?

Violetta—Cielo!—egli è vero! (da sè.)
Il vedo.

Barone—Da voi non un sol detto si volga
(piano a VIOLETTA.)
a questo Alfredo!

Violetta—Ah, perchè venni incauta! Pietà
(da sè.)
di me, gran Dio!

Flora—Meco t' assidi; narrami — quai novità vegg' io?

(A VIOLETTA, facendola sedere presso dis è sul divano. Il DOTTORE si avvicina ad esse, che commessamente conversano. Il MARCHESE si trattiene a parte col BARONE; GASTONE taglia; ALFREDO ed altri puntano altri passegiano.

Alfredo—Un quattro!

Gastone—Ancora hai vinto!

Alfredo—Sfortuna nell' amore vale fortuna giuoco.
(punta e vince.)

Tutti—E sempre vincitore!

Alfredo—Oh, vincerò stassera; e l' oro guadagnato
Poscia a goder fra' campi ritornerò beato.

Flora—Solo?

Alfredo—No, no con tale, che vi fu meco ancor,
Poi mi sfuggìa.
(da sè.)

Violetta—Mio Dio!
(ad ALFREDO indic. VIOLETTA.)

Gastone—Pietà di lei.
(ad ALFREDO, con mal frenata ira.)

Barone—Signor!
(piano al BARONE)

Violetta—Frenatevi, o vi lascio.
(disinvolto.)

Alfredo—Barone, m'appellaste?
(ironico.)

Barone—Siete in si gran fortuna,
Che al gioco mi tentaste.

Alfredo—Sì!—la disfida accetto.

Violetta—Che fia?—morir mi sento!
(da sè.)
Pietà, gran Dio, di me!
(punta.)

Barone—Cento luigi a destra.
(punta.)

Alfredo—Ed alla manca cento.
(ad ALFREDO).

Gastone—Un asso—un faute—hai vinto!

(to ALFRED).

Baron—Wilt double?

Alfred—A double be it.

(dealing off).

Gaston—A four-spot—a seven.

Alfred—Then I'm again victorious.

All—Bravely indeed! good fortune seems partial to Alfred!

Flora—Ah! for the rustic dwelling the Baron pays expenses.

(to the BARON).

Alfred—Now we'll go on!

(entering).

Servant—The banquet is ready!

Flora—Let's go then.

(starting.)

All—Let's go then.

(to the BARON).

Alfred—Shall we our game continue?

Baron—At present, no, we cannot;
Ere long, my losses I'll regain.

Alfred—At any game that suits you.

Baron—Our friends we'll follow. After—

Alfred—Whene'er you call, you'll find me.

(All retire through a door in the center—the stage left empty for a moment).

SCENE XIII—VIOLETTA returns, breathless, followed by ALFRED.

Violetta—I have asked him to come hither.
Will he do so? And will he hear me?
Yes, he will, for bitter hate
Controls him more than my sad accents.

Alfred—Didst thou call me? What dost wish for?

Violetta—Quickly leave this place, I pray you;
Danger o'er you is suspended.

Alfred—Ah! you're clearly comprehended.
E'en so base you then believe me?

Violetta—Ah no, no, never!

Alfred—But what then fear you?

Violetta—Ah, I fear the Baron's fury.

Alfred—An affair of death's between us;
Should this hand in death extend him,
One sole blow would then deprive thee
Both of lover and protector;
Would such losses sorrow give thee?

Violetta—But if he should prove the victor!
There behold the sole misfortune,
That, I fear, would prove me fatal.

Alfred—Pray, what care you for my safety?

Violetta—Hence, depart now, this present instant!

Alfred—I will go, but swear this moment,
Thou wilt follow now and ever,
Where I wander.

Violetta—Ah, no; never.

Alfred—No! and never!

Barone—Il doppio?

Alfredo—Il doppio sia.

(tagliando.)

Gastone—Un quattro, un sette—

Tutti—Ancora!

Alfredo—Pur la vittoria è mia!

Coro—Bravo davver!—la sorte è tutta per Alfredo!

Flora—Del villeggia la spesa farà il Baron già lo vedo.

(al BARONE.)

Alfredo—Seguite pur!

Serve—La cena è pronta.

Flora—Andiamo.

(avviandosi.)

Coro—Andiamo.

(tra loro a parte.)

Alfredo—Se continuar v' aggrada—

Barone—Per ora nol possiamo.
Più tardi la rivincita.

Alfredo—Al gioco che vorrete.

Barone—Seguiam gli amici; poscia

Alfredo—Sarò qual mi vorrete.

(Tutti entrano nella porta di mezzo: la scena rimane un istante vuota.)

SCENA XIII—VIOLETTA, che ritorna affannata, indi ALFREDO.

Violetta—Invitato a qui seguirmi,
Verrà desso?—vorrà udirmi?
El verrà—chè l' odio atroce
Puote in lui più di mia voce.

Alfredo—Mi chiamaste?—Che bramate?

Violetta—Questi luoghi abbandonate—
Un periglio vi sovrasta.

Alfredo—Ah, comprendo!—Basta, basta—
E sì vile mi credete?

Violetta—Ah, no, mai.

Alfredo—Me che temete?

Violetta—Tremo sempre del Barone.

Alfredo—E tra noi mortal quistione—
S' ei cadrà per mano mia
Un sol colpo vi torria
Coll' amante il protettore—
V' atterrisce tal sciagura?

Violetta—Ma s' ei fosse l' uccisore!—
Ecco l' unica sventura—
Ch' io pavento a me fatale!

Alfredo—La mia morte!—Che ven cale?

Violetta—Deh, partite, e sull' istante.

Alfredo—Partirò, ma giura innante
Che dovunque seguirai
I miei passi.

Violetta—Ah no, giammai.

Alfredo—No!—giammai!

Violetta—Go, thou, unhappy! and forget me.
Thus degraded, go and leave me!
At this moment, to escape thee
I a sacred oath have taken!

Alfred—To hom? tell me! who could claim it?

Violetta—One who had the right to name it.

Alfred—'Twas Dauphol?
(with great effort).

Violetta—Yes.

Alfred—Then thou lov'st him.

Voiletta—Ah, well, I love him.
(Runs furiously, throws open the doors and cries out:)

Alfred—Come hither all!

SCENE XIV—The same, and all the others, who enter in confusion.

All—Did you call us? Now what would you?
(pointing to VIOLETTA, who leans fainting against the table).

Alfred—Know ye all this woman present?

All—Who? Violetta?

Alfred—Know ye, too, her base misconduct?

Violetta—Ah! spare me!

All—No!

Alfred—All she possessed, this woman here
Hath for my love expended.
I blindly, basely wretchedly,
This to accept, condescended.
But there is time to purge me yet
From stains that shame, confound me.
Bear witness all around me
That witness I pay the debt.

(In a violent range he throws a purse at VIOLETTA's feet—she faints in the arms of FLORA and the DOCTOR. At this moment Alfred's father enters).

SCENE XV—The same, and GERMONT, the lder, who has entered at the last words

All—Oh, to what baseness thy passions have moved thee.
To wound thus fatally one who has loved thee!
Shameless traducer of woman defenseless,
Depart hence, speedily, scorned and despised,

Germont—O scorn most worthy himself doth render
Who wounds in anger a woman tender!
My son, where is he? No more I see him;
In thee, Alfred, I seek him, but in vain.
(aside).

Alfred—Ah! yes, 'twas shameful! a deed, abhorrent,
A jealous fury—love's maddening torrent
Oppressed my senses, destroyed my reason;
From her, no pardon shall I obtain!
To fly and leave her, strength was denied me,
My angry passions did hither guide me.
But now that fury is all expended

Violetta—Va, sciagurato,
Scorda un nome ch' è infamato—
Va—mi lascia sul momento—
Di fuggirti un giuramento
Sacro io feci.

Alfredo—E chi potea?

Violetta—Chi diritto pien ne avea.

Alfredo—Fu Douphol?
(con supremo sforzo.)

Violetta—Sì.

Alfredo—Dunque l'ami?

Violetta—Ebben—l'amo.
(corre mirente sulla porta, e grida:)

Alfredo—Or tutti a me

SCENA XIV—Detti, e TUTTI i precedenti, che confusamente ritornano.

Tutti—Ne appellaste?—Che volete?
(additando VIOLETTA che abbattuta si appeggia al tavolino.)

Alfredo—Questa donna conoscete?

Tutti—Chi? Violetta?

Alfredo—Che facesse
Non sepete?

Violetta—Ah, taci.

Tutti—No.

Alfredo—Ogni suo aver tal femina
Per amor mio sperdea.
Io cieco, vile, misero,
Tutto accettar potea,
Ma, è tempo ancora! tergermi,
Da tanta macchia bramo
Qui testimon vi chiamo
Che qui pagato io l'ho!

(ALFREDO getta con furente sprezzo il ritratto di VIOLETTA ai piedi di lei, ed essa sviene tra le braccia di FLORA e del DOTTORE In tal momento entra il Padre.)

SCENA XV—Detti, ed il Signor GERMONT, ch' entra all' ultime parole.

Tutti—Oh, infamia orribile tu commettesti!—
Un cor sensibile così uccidesti!—
Di donne ignobile insulatatore,
Di qua allontanati, ne desti orror.

Germont—Di sprezzo degno sè stesso rende.
Chi pur nell' ira la donna offende.
Dov' è mio figlio?—Più non lo vedo.
In te più Alfredo—trovar non so.

(da se.)

Alfredo—Ah, sì!—che feci!—ne sento orrore!
Gelosa smania, deluso amore
Mi starzian l'alma—più non ragiono—
Da lei perdono—più non avro.
Volea fuggirla—non ho potuto!—
Dall' ira spinto, son qui venuto!—
Or che lo sdegno ho disfogato.
Me sciaguarato!—rimorso io n' ho.

(aside).

Germont—I 'mid them only know what bright
    virtues
    Dwell in that sad heart so torn and bleeding.
    I know she loves him all else unheeding;
    Yet must, tho cruel, silent remain.

Gaston } Oh! thou dost suffer! but cheer thy
Flora }   heart
    Here in thy trials we all take part.
    Kind friends surround thee, care o'er thee
    keeping,
    Cease then thy weeping thy tears restrain.

Baron—This shameful insult against this lady
    Offends all present; behold me ready
    To punish outrage! Here now declaring
    Such pride o'erbearing I will restrain.

(reviving).

Violetta—Ah, loved Alfred, this heart's devotion
    Thou canst not fathom yet—its fond emotion!
    Thou'rt still unknowing that at the measure
    Of this displeasure, 'tis proved again.
    But when, hereafter, the truth comes over
    thee,
    And my affection shall rise before thee,
    May Heav'n in pity then spare thee remorse.
    Ah, tho' dead, still loving, ever will I remain!

(GERMONT takes his son with him; the BARON follows;
VIOLETTA is taken into an adjoining room by the Doctor
and FLORA, and the rest disperse.

END OF THE SECOND ACT.

ACT III.

SCENE I—VIOLETTA's bedroom. At the back a bed,
with the curtains partly drawn. A window shut by in-
side shutters. Near the bed a table with a bottle of
water, a crystal cup, and different kinds of medicine
on it. In the middle of the room a toilet-table and
settee; a little apart from which is another piece of
furniture, upon which a night-lamp is burning. Chairs
and other articles of furniture. On the left a fireplace
with a fire in it.

(VIOLETTA discovered sleeping on the bed—ANNINA,
seated near the fireplace, has fallen asleep.)

Violetta—Annina!   awaking).

Annina—Did you call me?
    (waking up, confusedly).

Violetta—Poor creature, were you sleeping?

Annina—Yes, but forgive me.

Violetta—Bring me here some water.
    (ANNINA does so).
    Look out now—is it yet daylight?

Annina—It is seven.

Violetta—To a little light give access.

(ANNINA opens the blinds, and looks into the street).

Annina—Doctor Grenvil has come—

Violetta—A friend most faithful!
    I wish to rise, assist me!

(She rises, but fals again—then, supported by AN-
NINA, she walks slowly towards the settee, and the
Doctor enters in time to assist her to sit upon it—
ANNINA places cushions about her.

SCENE II—The same, and the Doctor

Violetta—How kind in you thinking of me thus
    early.

Doctor—Yes, are you somewhat better?
    (feeling her pulse).

(da se.)

Germont—Io sol fra tutti so qual virtude
    Di quella misera il sen racchiude—
    Io so che l'ama, che gli è fedele;
    Eppur, crudele, tacer dovrò!

Gastone } Oh quanto peni! ma pur fi cor
Flora } Quì soffre ognuno del tuo dolor;
    Fracari amici qui sei soltanto,
    Rascinga il pianto che t' inondò.

Barone—A questa donna l' atroce insulto
    Qui tutti offese ma non inulto
    Fia tanto oltraggio! Provar vi voglio
    Che il vostro orgoglio fiaccar saprò!

(riavendosi.)

Violetta—Alfredo, Alfredo, di questo core
    Non puoi comprendere tutto l'amore;
    Tu non conosci che fino a prezzo
    Del tuo disprezzo—provato io l' ho!
    Ma verrà giorno, in che il saprai—
    Com' io t'amassi confesserai—
    Dio dai rimorsi ti salvi allora
    Io penta ancora—pur t'amero.

(GERMONT trae seco il figlio; il BARONE lo
segue VIOLETTA è condotta in altra stanza dal
DOTTORE e da FLORA; gli altri si disperdano.)

FINE DELL' ATTO SECONDO.

ATTO III.

SCENA I—Camera da letto di VIOLETTA. Nel
fondo e un letto con cortine mezzo tirate; una
finestra chiusa da imposte interne; presso il letto
uno sgabello su cui una bottiglia d'acqua, una
tazza di cristallo, diverse medicine. A metà della
scena una toilette, vicino un canapè; più distante
un altro mobile, su cui arde un lume da notte,
varie sedie ed altri mobili. La porta è a sinistra;
di fronte v' è n caminetto con fuoco acceso.

(VIOLETTA dorme sul letto—ANNINA, seduta
presso il caminetto, è pure addormita.)

Violetta—Annina!   (destandosi.)

Annina—Comandate?
    (svegliandosi confusa.)

Violetta—Dormivi, poveretta?

Annina—Sì, perdonate.

Violetta—Dammi d' acqua un sorso.
    (ANNANA esequisce)
    Osserva, è pieno il giorno?

Annina—Son sett' ore.

Violetta—Dà accesso a un pò di luce.
    (Apre le imposte, e guarda nella via.)

Annina—Il Signor Grenvil!

Violetta—Oh, il vero amico!—
    Alzar mi vo'—m'aita.

(Si alza e ricade; ol sostenuta da ANNINA va
lentamente verso il canapè, ed il DOTTORE entra
in tempo per assisterla ad adagiarvisi—ANNANA
vi aggiunge dei cuscini.)

SCENA II—Dette, ed il DOTTORE.

Violetta—Quanta bontà!—Pensaste a me
    per tempo!

Dottore—Or come vi sentite?
    (le tocca il poso.)

Violetta—With pain I suffer; but my mind is tranquil.

A priest came here last evening and brought me comfort.

Ah! religion is a solace to us in affliction.

Doctor—Last night, how were you?

Violetta—Calmly I slept till morning.

Doctor—Then keep your courage.

Convalescence, haply, is not far distant.

Violetta—Oh! that's a kind of deception Allowed to all physicians.

(pressing her hand).

Doctor—Farewell now. I'll return soon.

Violetta—Be not forgetful.

(in a low tone, whilst following the Doctor).

Annina—Is her case more hopeful?

Doctor—But few brief hours of life are to her remaining.

(departs).

SCENE III—Violetta and Annina.

Annina—Now cheer thy heart.

Violetta—Is this a festal morning?

Annina—Paris gives up to folly—'tis carnival day.

Violetta—Ah, 'mid this gay rejoicing, Heav'n alone doth know

How the poor are suffering! What amount Is there in that casket?

(opens and counts).

Annina—Just twenty louis'.

Violetta—Take from it ten, and give them to the needy.

Annina—Little you'll have remaining.

(sighing).

Violetta—Oh, 'twill for me be plenty! You can bring then my letters here.

Annina—But you?

Violetta—Naught will occur. You need not long be absent.

(exit Annina).

SCENE IV—Violetta takes a letter from her bosom and reads:

"Thou hast kept thy promise. The duel took place. The Baron was wounded, but is improving. Alfred is in foreign countries. Your sacrifice has been revealed to him by me. He will return to you for pardon. I too will return. Haste to recover, thou deservest a bright future.

"Georgio Germont."

Violetta—'Tis too late!

Still watching and waiting, but to me they come not!

(looking in the mirror).

Oh, how I'm changed and faded!

But the Doctor doth exhorted me to be hopeful;

Ah! thus afflicted, all hope is dead within me!

Violetta—Soffre il mio corpo, ma tranquilla ho l'alma.

Mi confortò ier sera un pio ministro.

Religione è sollievo a' sofferenti.

Dottore—E questa notte?

Violetta—Ebbi tranquillo il sonno.

Dottore—Coraggio adunque — la convalescenza

Non è lontana.

Violetta—Oh, la bugia pietosa A' medici è concessa.

(stringendole la mano.)

Dottore—Addio—a più tardi.

Violetta—Non mi scordate.

(piano al Dottor, accompagnandolo.)

Annina—Come va, Signore?

Dottore—La tisi non le accorda che poch' ore.

(Piano, e parte.)

SCENA III—Violetta ed Annina.

Annina—Or fate cor.

Violetta—Giorno di festa è questo?

Annina—Tutta Parigi impazza—è carnevale.

Violetta—Oh, nel comun tripudio, sallo il cielo

Quanti infelici gemon!—Quale somma V' ha in quello stipo?

(indicandolo.)

(l'apre e conta.)

Annina—Venti luigi.

Violetta—Dieci ne reca ai poveri tu stessa.

Annina—Poco rimanvi allora.

Violetta—Oh, mi sarà bastante

(sospirando.)

Cerca poscia mie lettere.

Annina—Ma voi?

Violetta—Nulla occorrà, sollecita, se puoi.

(Annina esce.)

SCENA IV—Violetta, che trae dal seno una lettera, e legge.

"Teneste la promessa—La disfida ebbe luogo; il Barone fu ferito, però migliora Alfredo è in stranio suolo; il vostro sacrifizio io stesso gli ho svelato. Egli a voi tornerà pel suo perdono; io pur verrò—Curatevi—mertaste un avvenir migliore.

"Georgio Germont."

Violetta—E tardi!—

(desolata.)

Attendo, attendo—Nè a me giungon mai?

(si guarda nello specchio.)

Oh, come son mutata!—

Ma il Dottore a sperar pure m' esorta!—

Ah, con tal morbo ogni speranza è morta.

LA TRAVIATA

ADDIO DEL PASSATO—*FAREWELL TO THE BRIGHT VISIONS* (Violetta)

Ad - di - o del pas - sa - to bei sog - ni ri - den - ti, le
Fare - well to the bright vis - ions I once fond - ly cher - ish'd, Al -

ro - se del vol - to gia so - no pal - len - ti l'a - mo - re d'Al
read - y the ro - ses that deck'd me have per - ish'd, The love of Al

fre - do per - fi - no mi man - ca, con - for - to, so - ste - gno dell'
fre - do is lost, past re - gain - ing, That cheer'd me when faint - ing, my

a - ni - ma stan - ca, con - for - to, so -
spir - it sus - tain - ing, sole com - fort, suf -

ste - gno ah! del - la tra - via - ta sor - ri - di al de - si - o, a
fort, ah! Pi - ty the stray one, and send her con - so - la - tion, Oh,

le - i deh per - do - na tu ac - co - gli - la o Di - o! ah! tut - to
par - don her trans - gress - ions, and grant her sal - va - tion. Ah! thus all

— tut - to fi - ni, or tut - to, tut - to fi - ni.
— of life doth end, Ah! thus all of life doth end.

The sorrows and enjoyments of life will soon be over,
The dark tomb in oblivion this mortal form will cover!
No flowers for my grave, no kind friends o'er me weeping.
No cross, with my name, mark the spot where I'm sleeping.
Ah, pity the stray one, and send her consolation!
Oh, pardon her transgressions, and send her salvation.
Thus all of life doth end.

(sits down).

BACCHANALIAN CHORUS (outside).
Room for the prize-ox, with honors appearing!
Gay flowers and vine-leaves in garlands he's wearing.

Le gioie, i dolori fra poco avran fine;
La tomba al mortali di tutto è confine!—
Non lagrima o fiore avrà la mia fossa,
Non corce, col nome, che copra quest' ossa!—
Ah, della traviata sorridi al desio,
A lei, deh perdona, tu accoglila, o Dio!
Or tutto finì.

(Siede.)

CORO BACCANTE (esterno.)

Largo al quadrupede sir della festa
Dio fiori e pampini cinto la testa—
Largo al più docile d' ogni cornuto

Room for the gentlest one of like creation,
Give him, with fife and horn loud salu-
    tation.
Now, Parisians, make concession.
Clear the way for our procession.

Asia or Africa ne'er saw one to beat him!
He is the proud boast of all those who
    meet him.
Maskers and merry boys with fun o'erflowing,
Songs in his honor raise, plaudits bestowing.
Now, Parisians, etc.

SCENE V—VIOLETTA, and ANNINA, returning hastily.
    (hesitating).

Annina—My lady—

Violetta—What has happened?

Annina—This morning—'tis true then? You are
    really better?

Violetta—Yes; but why?

Annina—Will you promise to be tranqquil?

Violetta—Yes, what wouldst tell me?

Annina—I would now prepare you
    For a pleasure unexpected.

Violetta—For a pleasure, thou sayest?

Annina—Yes, gentle mistress.

Violetta—Alfred! Ah, thou hast seen him!
    He comes! oh, haste thee!
(ANNINA makes signs with her hand in the affirma-
tive, and goes to open the door.)

SCENE VI—VIOLETTA, ALFRED, and ANNINA.
    (Going towards the door).

Violetta—Alfred

Alfred—
(ALFRED enters, pale with emotion, and they throw
themselves into each others' arms, exclaiming:)

Violetta—Beloved Alfred!

Alfred—My own Violetta!
    Ah, I am guilty! I know all, dearest.

Violetta—I only know, love, that thou art
    near me!

Alfred—This throbbing heart will show how
    I still love thee.
    I could no more exist, if from thee parted.

Violetta—If thou hast found me yet with the
    living,
    Believe that grief and woe no more can kill

Alfred—Forget the sorrow in love forgiving,
    Both sire and son thou'lt pardon still.

Violetta—Ask me for pardon? 'Tis I am guilty,
    Thus rendered by my loving heart.

Both—No earthly power, nor friend, beloved,
    Shall tear us hence apart.

Violetta—Ah, no more! to church let us be going,
    Our thanks to render with hearts o'erflowing.
         (Staggers.)

Alfred—Thou'rt growing pale!

Di corni e pifferi abbia il saluto.
Parigini, date passo al trionfo del Bue
    grasso
L' Asia, nè L' Africa vide il più bello,
Vanto ed orgoglio d' ogni macello—
Allegre maschere, pazzi garzoni,
Tutti plauditello con canti e suoni!—
Parigini, etc.—

SCENA V—Detta, ed ANNINA, che torna fret-
tolosa.

Annina—Signora—   (esitando.)

Violetta—Che t' accadde?

Annina—Quest oggi, è vero! vi sentite
    meglio?

Violetta—Sì; perchè?

Annina—D' esser calma promettete?

Violetta—Si; che vuoi dirmi?

Annina—Prevenir vi volli—
    Una gioia improvvisa.

Violetta—Una gioia!—dicesti?

Annina—Si, o Signora.

Violetta—Alfredo!—Ah, tu il vedesti!
    Ei vien! l' affretta.
(ANNINA afferma col capo, e va ad aprire la
    porta.)

SCENA VI—VIOLETTA, ALFREDO ed ANNINA.
    (andando verso l' uscio.)

Violetta—Alfredo?—

Alfredo
(Comparisce, pallido pella commozione, ed am-
bidue get tandosi le braccia al collo, esclamano:)

Violetta—Amato Alfredo!

Alfredo—Mia Violetta!—
    Colpervol sono—so tutto, o cara—

Violetta—Io so che alfine reso mi sei.

Alfredo—Da questo palpito, s' io t'ami,
    impara—
    Senza te esistere più non potrei.

Violetta—Ah, s'anco in vita m' hai
    ritrovata,
    Credi, che uccidere non può il dolor.

Alfredo—Scorda l'affanno, donna adorata.
    A me perdona e al genitor.

Violetta—Ch' io ti perdoni?—La rea son io?
    Ma solo amore tal mi rendè.

Alfredo e Violetta—Null' uomo o demone,
    angelo mio.
    Mai più staccarti portà da me.

Violetta—Ah, non più—a un tempio—
    Alfredo, andiamo,
    Del tuo ritorno grazie rendiamo.
         (Vacilla.)

Violetta—'Tis nothing, mark me; unlooked for pleasure can never enter
   Without disturbing a heart o'erburdened.

(She sinks on a chair fainting, and her head falls backwards.)

Alfred—Great Heaven!—Violetta!

   (Alarmed, and supporting her.)

Violetta—'Tis but the weakness
   From recent illness. Now, love, I'm stronger—
      (With effort)
   See'st thou? and smiling—

Alfred—(Ah, cruel fortune!)

Violetta—'Twas nothing! Annina, a shawl bring hither.

Alfred—What now, love? but wait then—

Violetta—No! I will go now.

(ANNINA presents the shawl, which she makes an effort to put on, but finds she is too weak, and exclaims:)

   Great Heav'n, I cannot.

(She throws away the shawl vexedly, and sinks again on the chair.)

Alfred—Heavens, what is it!
   Go, call the Doctor.

      (to ANNINA).

Violetta—Ah, tell him—say that Alfred is now beside me.
   Return'd and faithful to my affection—
   Tell him I wish still to live.
      (ANNINA returns.)
      (to ALFRED).
   But though returned, love, thou hast not saved me.
   No earthly power from the tomb can shield me.

SCENE VII—VIOLETTA and ALFRED.

Violetta—Ah, cruel fate to die so young,
   Tho, much I've borne of sorrow.
   To die when hopes, to which I clung,
   Reveal a brighter morrow!
   Ah! then 'twas naught but madness.
   The love to which I yielded!
   In vain my heart was shielded,
   Armed with faith, all, all in vain.

Alfred—Oh, dearer far than breath or life,
   Beloved one, fondly treasured!
   My burning tears, in this dark hour,
   With thine shall flow, unmeasured.
   But, ah! far more than e'er before
   I need thy fond devotion;
   Yield not to sad emotion
   While hope doth still remain!

(VIOLETTA throws herself upon the lounge.)

SCENE THE LAST—The same, GERMONT, and the Doctor.

Germont—Ah, Violetta—   (entering).

Violetta—You, my friend?

Alfred—My father—

Violetta—Thou'st not forgot me?

Germont—I redeem my promise—
   And come, thou noble hearted,
   As my daughter to embrace thee.

Alfredo—Tu impallidisci!

Violetta—E nulla, sai? Gioja improvvisa non entra mai,

(S' abbandona, come sfinita, sopra una sedia, col capo pendente all' indietro.)

Alfredo—Gran Dio!—Violetta!

   (Spaventato, sorreggendola)

Violetta—E il mio malore.
   Fe debolezza—ora son forte—
   Vedi?—sorrido.

      (sforzandosi.)

Alfredo—(Ah, cruda sorte!)

Violetta—Fu nulla—Annina, dammi a vestire.

Alfredo—Adesso!—Attendi.

Violetta—No—voglio uscire.

(ANNINA le presenta una vesta ch'ella fa per indossare, e impeditane dalla debolezza, esclama:)

   Gran Dio!—non posso!

(getta con dispetto la veste, e ricade sulla sedia.)

Alfredo—Cielo, che vedo!
   Va pel Dottore.

      (ad ANNINA.)

Violetta—Digli che Alfredo
   E ritornato all' amor mio—
   Digli che vivere ancor vogl' io.
      (ANNINA parte.)
      (ad ALFREDO.)
   Ma se tornando non m'hai salvato.
   A niuno in terra salvarmi è dato.

SCENA VII—VIOLETTA ed ALFREDO.

Violetta—Gran Dio! morir sì giovane,
   Io, che penato ho tanto!
   Morir si presso a tergere
   Il mio si lungo pianto!
   Ah, dunque fu delirio
   La credula speranza;
   Invano di costanza
   Armato aurò il mio cor!
Alfredo—oh, fil crudo termine
   Serbato al nostro amor!

Alfredo—Oh, mio sospiro,—oh, palpito
   Diletto del cor mio!
   Le mie colle tue lagrime
   Confondere degg' io—
   Or più che mai nostr' anime
   Han duopo di costanza—
   Ah, tutto alla speranza
   Non chiudere il tuo cor!
   Violetta mia, deh calmati,
   M' uccide il tuo dolor.

(VIOLETTA s'abbandona sul canapè.)

SCENA ULTIMA—Detti, GERMONT, ed i DOTTORE.

Germont—Ah, Violetta!   (entrando.)

Violetta—Voi, signor!

Alfredo—Mio padre !

Violetta—Non mi scordaste?

Germont—La promessa adempio—
   A stringervi qual figlia vengo al seno,
   O generosa.